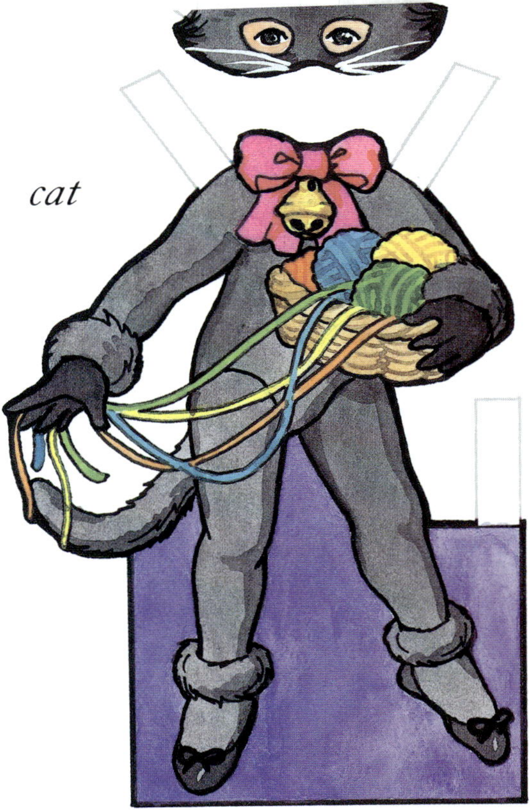

cat

monster

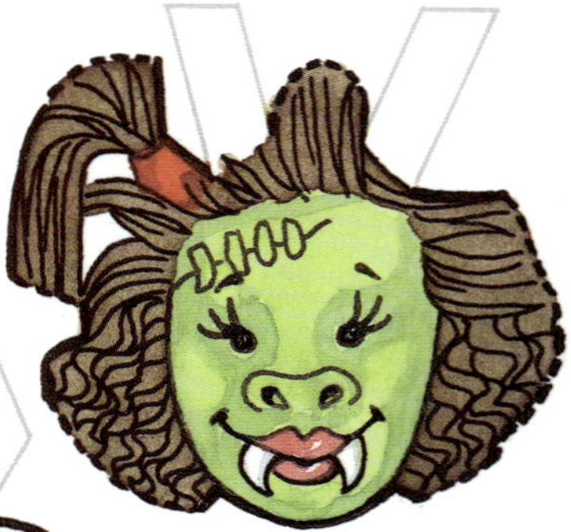

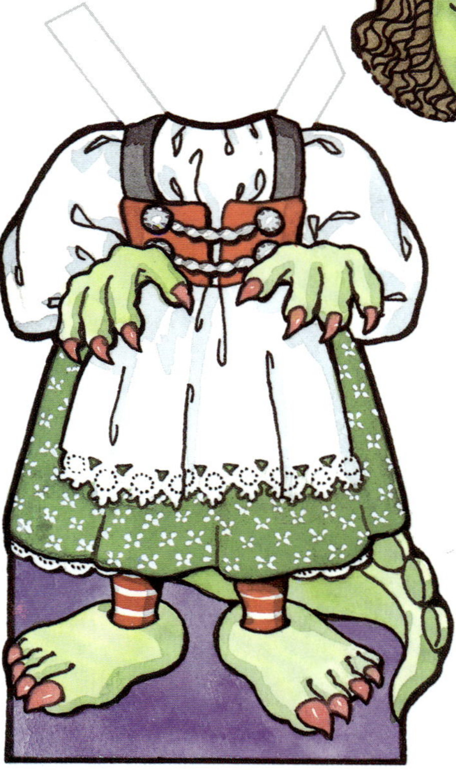

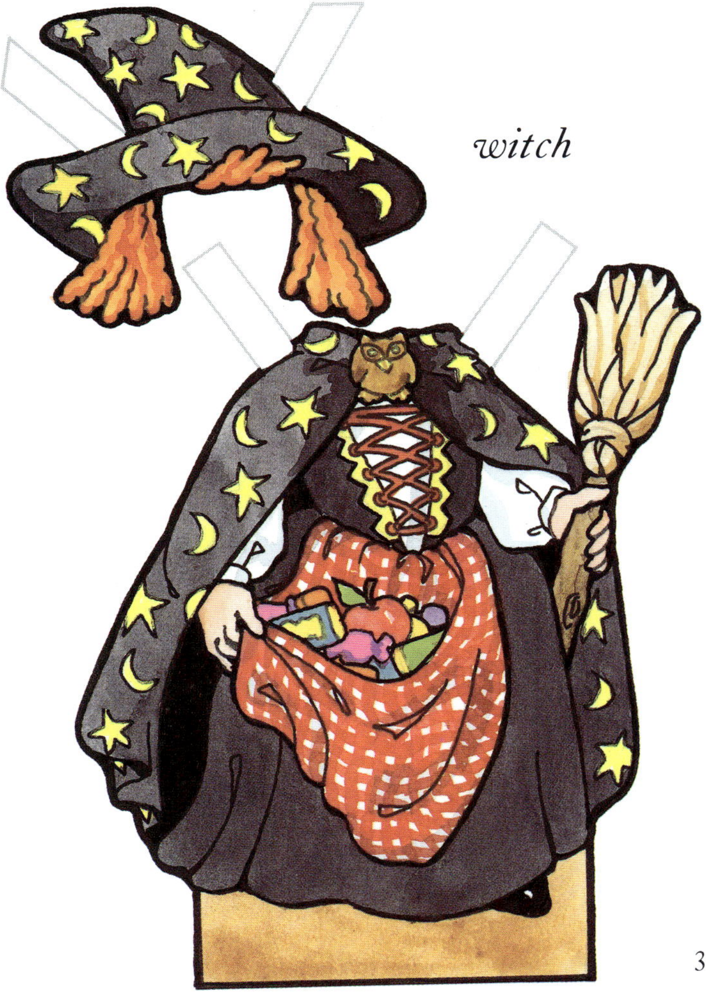

witch

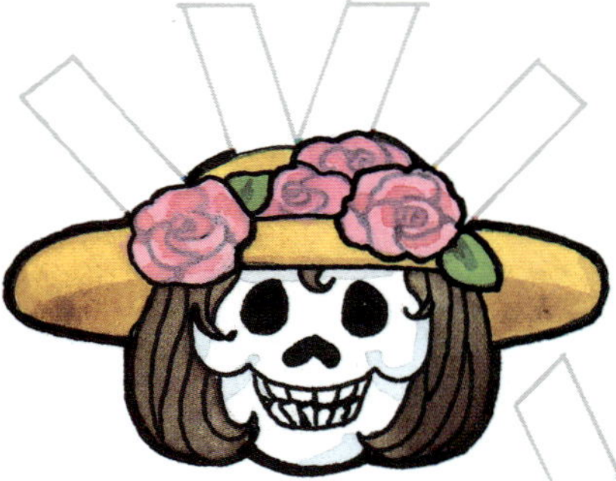

skeleton

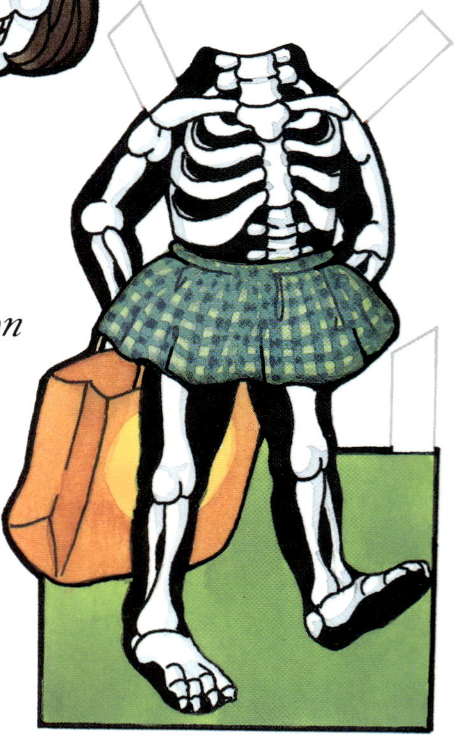

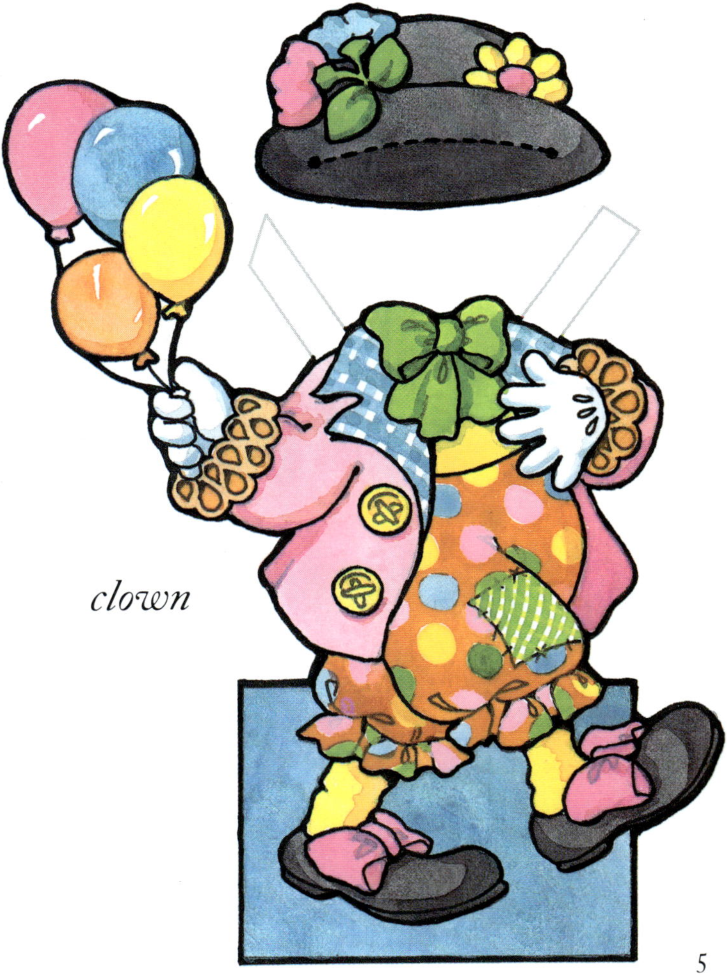

clown

pirate

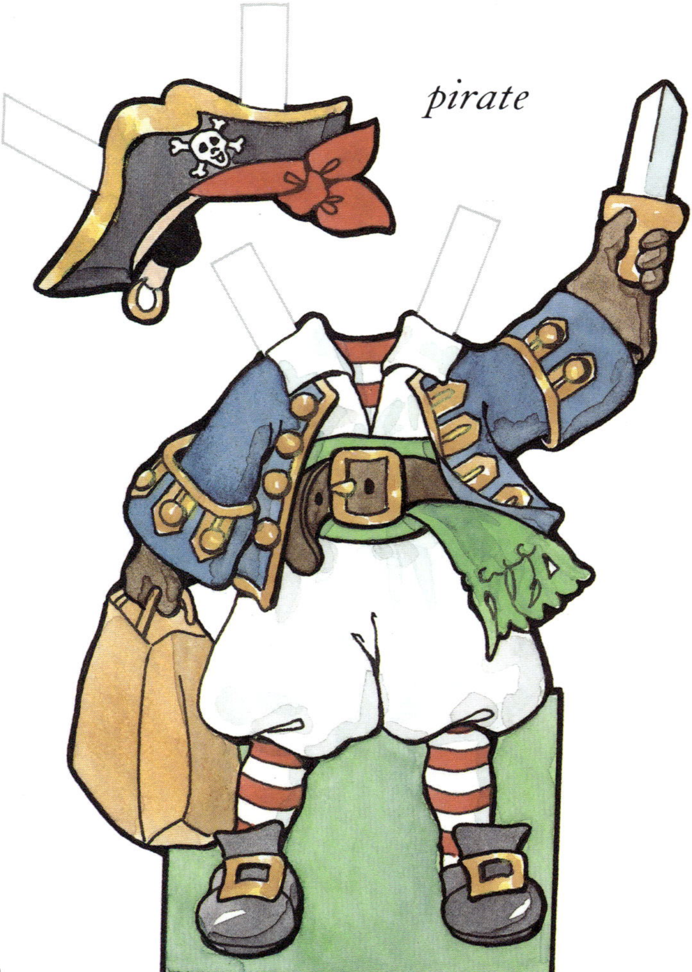

gypsy

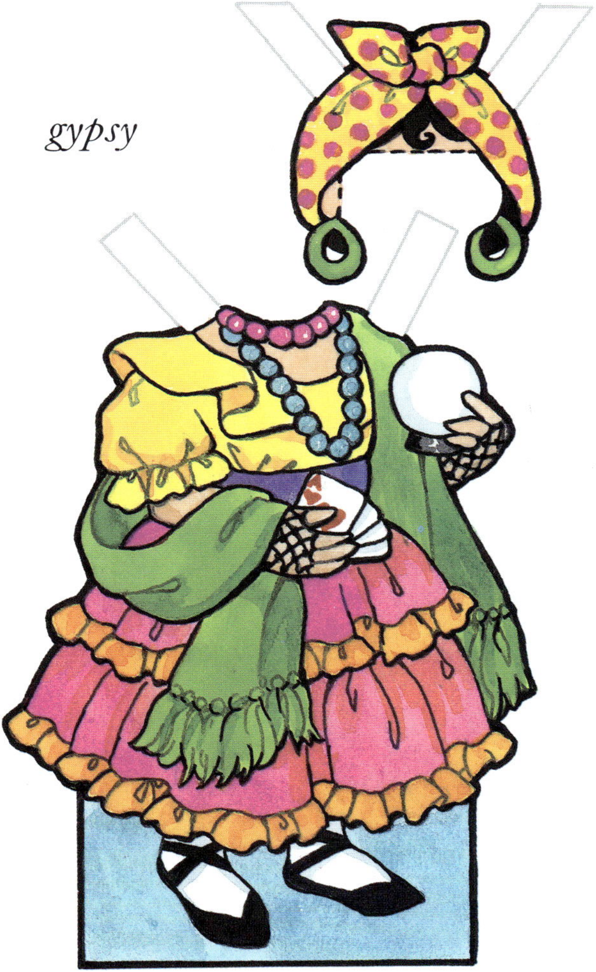

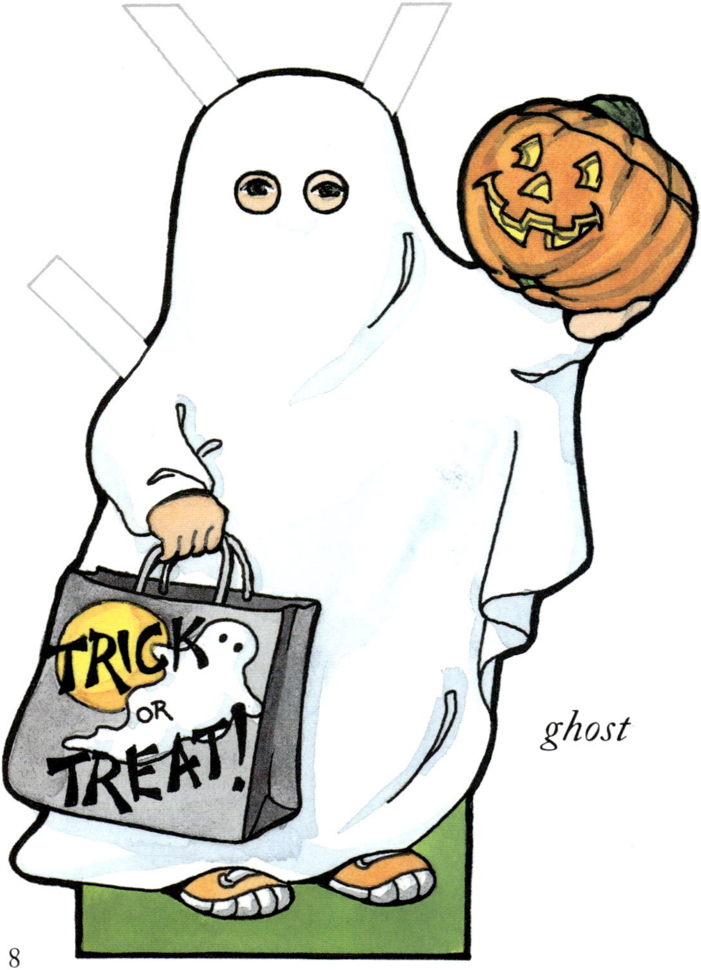

ghost

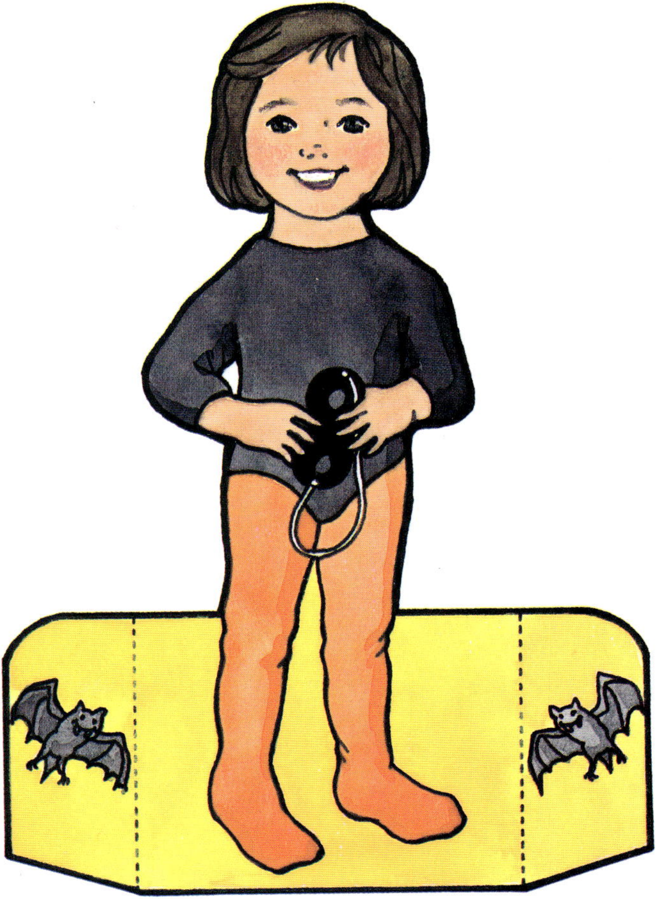

ISBN 0-486-26053-4

90000

$1.00 IN USA
$1.50 IN CANADA

9 780486 260532